THE GREATEST SHOW ON TURF

THE GREATEST SHOW ON TURF

THE STORY OF 99-01 ST. LOUIS RAMS

ROBERT MULLEN

**Outkirts Press, Inc.
Denver, Colorado**

The opinions expressed in this manuscript are solely the opinions of the author and do not represent the opinions or thoughts of the publisher. The author has represented and warranted full ownership and/or legal right to publish all the materials in this book.

The Greatest Show On Turf
The story of 99-01 St. Louis Rams
All Rights Reserved.
Copyright © 2009 Robert Mullen
v1.0

Cover Photo © 2009 JupiterImages Corporation. All rights reserved - used with permission.

This book may not be reproduced, transmitted, or stored in whole or in part by any means, including graphic, electronic, or mechanical without the express written consent of the publisher except in the case of brief quotations embodied in critical articles and reviews.

Outskirts Press, Inc.
http://www.outskirtspress.com

ISBN: 978-1-4327-4487-8

Outskirts Press and the "OP" logo are trademarks belonging to Outskirts Press, Inc.

PRINTED IN THE UNITED STATES OF AMERICA

Contents

The Greatest Show on Turf 7
'99 Season 13
'00 Season 17
'01 Season 19
Kurt Warner 25
Marshall Faulk 33
The Defense 39
Dick Vermeil 45
Mike Martz 49
Ricky Proehl 53
Az-Zahir Hakim/Tony Horne/Special Teams 57
Tony Horne 61
Isaac Bruce 63
Torry Holt 67
The Legacy 71

The Greatest Show on Turf

January 30th, 2000, in a packed Georgia Dome, 72,000 screaming fans await the final play of Super Bowl XXXIV. The Rams are hanging on to a 1-touchdown lead 23–16. At this point, the Rams' defense is absolutely exhausted from a long drive orchestrated by Steve McNair. McNair takes the snap and straight over the middle on a slant route Kevin Dyson is bolting. McNair releases the ball quickly into Dyson's hands. Dyson looks like he is headed for six, but suddenly, Mike Jones takes him down by the legs. Dyson stretches his arms as far as he can, but he is just a yard short. This would finalize the Rams' '99 season as one of the best ever. They proved by far they were the best offense ever assembled, averaging 35 points a game. They had MVP Kurt Warner and offensive MVP Marshall

◄ **THE GREATEST SHOW ON TURF**

Faulk and the fastest receivers in the league.

Year after year, watching the St. Louis Rams having mediocre to some very poor seasons, it's fun to think back and reminisce about "The Greatest Show On Turf." This label refers to the Rams from 1999–2001. It's a phrase coined by Chris Berman when he did *NFL Primetime* and covered the Rams' highlights. He comes up with many clever names, but why were the Rams compared to the Ringling Brothers' "Greatest Show On Earth"? The answer is simple: they were exciting; unpredictable; they made big plays; had extreme speed, especially when they played on turf because then, their game and speed were magnified.

In the Edward Jones Dome, formerly TWA Dome, no team could match their skill. They were 8–0 at home and never trailed by more than 7 points at home. They trailed for a total of 4:29 seconds at home that season. For a period of 3 years, no one had better offensive numbers than the St. Louis Rams. They were the only team in history to score 500 points in three consecutive seasons. They were arguably the fastest team ever assembled. Everything they did and every play they made was up-tempo. Not many people realize how good the '99 defense and the special teams were. They

THE GREATEST SHOW ON TURF

were always over shadowed by the explosive fast offense. They won Super Bowl XXXIV and made it to Super Bowl XXXVI, and lost on a last-second field goal.

I always think *what-if?* Would there have been a dynasty if they had won? Now, we talk about a Patriots' dynasty. Did that field goal change the fate of the St. Louis Rams? Perhaps they would have gone on to win more, but there is no use in thinking about *what-ifs*. It is what it is, and they are still an era worth mentioning.

I think around the time of the '99 draft, people may have thought the Rams would improve, but I don't think anybody saw this coming. Dick Vermeil, the head coach, was overemotional and was perhaps on the verge of another breakdown. He was on the hot seat as coach. He had one more year to prove himself after having 2 awful years with the Rams. Many thought he should have never come out of retirement.

Mike Martz, the offensive coordinator, was an offensive genius although not very well known at the time. He came off as arrogant and cocky. In the off-season, they acquired young quarterback Trent Green from the Redskins, and probably the best running back in the game at the time, Mar-

◄ **THE GREATEST SHOW ON TURF**

shall Faulk from the Colts. The offense had Isaac Bruce, who was already established as one of the better receivers in the game.

Then came the '99 draft, and they deserve a lot of credit for that draft. They picked up Torry Holt, who made the receiving duo deadly. Dré Bly was another good, notable draft pick on defense. He played as a nickel back that year and is now a premiere cornerback in the league. Those were the missing pieces that they put together, but little did anybody know that the biggest piece was not a starter on the depth chart. Quarterback Kurt Warner was the final piece added to complete this team.

If I had said that in 1998 or 1999 preseason, anybody would have asked, "Who the hell is Kurt Warner?" Warner played in one NFL game in '98 and played D-1A football for Northern Iowa, Arena League, NFL Europe, and, oh yeah, was working at Hy-Vee stocking shelves, hoping the NFL would call after two failed attempts in the NFL.

In a preseason game against the San Diego Chargers, Trent Green went down hard, hit in the back of the leg, and was out for the season. I can still remember the image of Isaac Bruce kneeling down at midfield, hands over his face, and he punched the field in anger. He was probably thinking to himself, "There goes the season."

I also recall the press conference shortly after, where Dick Vermeil was addressing the situation. He seemed like he had just got over crying, and he said, "We will rally around Kurt Warner, and we will play good football." I don't know what it is about watching that clip, but I get chills whenever I see that. How did he have such a gut feeling about the shelf stocker? Most coaches would have looked around the league for free agents, but he gambled and went with his gut.

'99 Season

Midway through preseason after suffering a major blow to the teams' offense, the hope in the city was diminished. Week 1 would be at home against the Baltimore Ravens. The Rams rolled right through the Ravens, winning an impressive 27–10. It was Kurt Warner's first career start, and no one expected much. He threw over 300 yards and 3 TDs. That would continue over the next few games.

Week 3 in Cincinnati, the hero was Az-Zahir Hakim, scoring 3 TDs on 3 receptions and an 84-yard punt return. As week 4 approached, the Rams got ready to face the San Francisco 49ers, the division bully. In the previous years, the 49ers would just absolutely beat down the Rams. The 49ers disrespected the Rams, referring to them as "the same

THE GREATEST SHOW ON TURF

old sorry-ass Rams." The Rams knew that the 49ers were always the team to beat in the NFC West. They dominated the 49ers 42–20, to improve the season to 4–0. Warner lit them up, throwing 5 TD passes. The kick returner Tony Horne had a huge day that impacted the game. With 4 returns, he had 199 yards and a touchdown.

Now at 4–0 and defeating the giant of the NFC West, there was a lot of buzz in the media about the Rams. *Sports Illustrated* published an article and cover story on Kurt Warner entitled, "Who Is This Guy?" The next two games were blowouts to improve to 6–0. Faulk rolled through the Falcons and Browns with a lot of rushing yards and receiving.

The next two games would bring the Rams back to earth. They played an away game against the Titans, their eventual Super Bowl opponent. The Rams came up just short against the Titans, and then the next week against the Lions. The Lions game was on a last-minute drive. At 6–2, many people believed they were just a fluke. The Rams would prove that to be false, as they were back to their winning ways.

Only at this point of the season did the defense start winning the games. The Rams' defense scored 2 TDs against Carolina, and then the following

'99 SEASON

week, another against the 49ers. They swept the 49ers for the first time in 19 years. Several weeks later, they defeated the Panthers again to clinch the division.

The offense was going strong at the beginning. Midseason, the defense picked up, and at the end of the season, they were firing on all cylinders. The Rams entered the playoffs 13–3 with home-field advantage throughout the playoffs. Their first game was quite a shoot-out against the Vikings, 49–37. The next game against the Tampa Bay Buccaneers was the exact opposite. It was a defensive struggle, but the Rams would prevail with 4 minutes left as Warner found Proehl in the end zone with an amazing throw and catch, to win 11–6. The aforementioned Super Bowl IV was an even better game than the NFC Championship. The Rams won on a 73-yard touchdown pass to Bruce and a defensive stop at the 1-yard line by Mike Jones as time expired.

'00 Season

The Rams looked poised to repeat the '99 season. This season was the first season with Mike Martz as head coach. They rolled through the first six games just like the season before. Every game was a blowout as the Rams scored 40 points in four out of the six contests, one time in the 50s and the other was in the high 30s. In that six-game stretch, Warner had all 300-yard passing games and 19 TDs. Although they were 6–0, something didn't seem right. The games were way out of hand, and it was obvious that they just couldn't rely on offense to outscore the other team every time.

Week 8 in Kansas City was the ultimate turning point of the season. The Chiefs thought they would struggle with the Rams' receivers; however, the natural grass and the fact that it rained pretty

◄ THE GREATEST SHOW ON TURF

hard slowed down the Rams. The Rams, this time, were on the other end of a blowout, losing 54–34. Kurt Warner broke his hand in the game, and this time, it was Trent Green's turn to take over. Green did well as the starter going 3–3, and together, the duo of Warner/Green combined 5,232 net yards, which still stand as an NFL team record. The real leader of the team was Marshall Faulk. He had an outstanding year, was the league MVP, and set a record of 26 total TDs.

In the wildcard round of the playoffs, the Rams faced the New Orleans Saints, a team that they had two great battles with during the season. The very last game of the season, they beat the Saints 26–21 to clinch the wildcard spot. The Rams had a chance to come back as they were down 31–7, and they scored 3 quick touchdowns, making the score 31–28.

The Rams were red-hot and had one last chance at a final drive as the Saints lined up to punt. Az Hakim muffed the punt at the 11-yard line, and the Saints recovered to win the game. That season had its successes and disappointments, but overall, it was a fairly good season. The Rams' front office knew that it was time to upgrade the defense the way they did the offense a few years ago.

'01 Season

The Rams, as expected, made a few changes to the defense, starting with a new defensive coordinator, Lovie Smith. With three first-round draft picks, they used them all on defense. They added Kim Herring from the Ravens, who was a part of the best defense in the league and was instrumental in their success. Their biggest acquisition, adding veteran Aeneas Williams, gave the defense a good leader.

For the third straight season, they went 6–0, including a 35–0 shutout against the Lions on a Monday night, embarrassing victories over the Dolphins and Jets, and a very exciting season opener against the Eagles that also ended in victory. Even with Faulk missing a couple of games, backup Trung Canidate made it unnoticeable that Faulk wasn't playing as he had two 100-plus-yard performances, including a 195-yard performance against the Jets.

In week 11, when they faced Tampa Bay, they had their hands full. This was starting to become a popular rivalry ever since their meeting in the playoffs 2 years prior to this. After a back and forth game, Warrick Dunn scored the game winning touchdown on a 21-yard run. After that game, the Rams would hit their stride and win six straight to finish their record at 14–2, one game better than their Super Bowl season.

The Rams looked primed to walk through the playoffs and get that second ring. The first challenge ahead of them in the playoffs was not much of a challenge. It was the Green Bay Packers, led by Brett Favre. The Rams' defense would make this probably Favre's worst performance of his long career. He threw his first interception early in the game to Aeneas Williams, who took it to the house to take the lead, 7–0.

The Rams would continue the beat-down on Favre as he threw two more interceptions that were returned for touchdowns—Tommy Polley scoring one and Williams scoring again. Favre threw six total interceptions, and the Packers turned over the ball eight times. Warner also threw a pair of touchdown passes, and Faulk ran one in, in a 45–17 blowout.

The NFC Championship Game against the Philadelphia Eagles was an interesting rematch from week 1. It was a bit back and forth, but the Eagles were hanging on to a slim lead at the half, 17–13. The Rams dominated the third quarter as the Eagles only had five offensive plays. First, the Rams hit a field goal to make the score 17–16. To take the lead, Torry Holt caught a 21-yard TD pass; however, the Rams went for a 2-point conversion so they could have a 1 touchdown lead, only they failed making the score 22–17 going into the fourth.

After holding the Eagles on the first two possessions of the fourth quarter, Faulk scored on a 1-yard TD run to make the score 29–17 with 6:55 remaining. But McNabb was far from done. The Eagles got possession after a good kick return by Brian Mitchell. McNabb completed a series of passes and would eventually run the ball in himself on a 3-yard scramble.

With the score 29–24, the Eagles forced the Rams to punt and had a chance to win on one last drive by the Eagles. On fourth and seven, McNabb delivered the pass to Freddie Mitchell, which was

◄ THE GREATEST SHOW ON TURF

picked off by none other than Aeneas Williams, to win the game. Aeneas Williams was proving to be a very clutch player during this playoff run.

They headed into the Super Bowl expecting no less than a ring. The odds in Las Vegas had the Rams as a 14-point favorite. I think people were expecting an uneventful Super Bowl, but it turned out quite the opposite. Midway through the first quarter, the Rams struck first, as expected, but only with a field goal. The Patriots responded quick with 2 touchdowns in the second quarter. One was an interception return by Ty Law, the other was a drive led by Brady that ended in an 8-yard TD pass to David Patten.

It was halftime, and St. Louis had never been down by more than 8 points the whole season. While losing 17–3 in the fourth, the Rams finally got things going as they drove to the Patriots' 1-yard line. On fourth down, Warner took it in on a sneak to make the game 17–10. The Rams were hot as they held the Patriots to a three and out and had one final chance to score as they started the drive at their own 46-yard line with 1:51 left.

Warner completed a series of passes and scored quickly when he found Proehl in the end zone. I recall Madden saying, "The Patriots should just take this game to overtime." I really wish they had, but Brady showed some heroics out there. He completed three passes in a row and then an incomplete. He made a few more completions and then spiked the ball at the 30-yard line, which set up the final play of the game. Adam Vinatieri came out and made a 48-yard field goal to win the game. I have had my heart broken before, but nothing compared to that moment.

It was a great effort and comeback for the Rams, and overall, an amazing season, but just a little short ...

Kurt Warner

There comes a time in every man's life where he will be put in a certain situation, whether he is ready or not. Kurt Warner was asked to head the St. Louis Rams through the 1999 season after a season-ending injury to Trent Green in a preseason game. Fans and players had no choice but to accept it. He answered the call more ready than anyone expected.

The first three games he threw for over 300 yards and 3 passing TDs, then came the Niners' game, and this would prove that the Rams are for real. The 49ers had dominated this division for years, and more importantly, dominated the Rams, beating them in 17 straight previous meetings. Warner thrashed the 49ers, throwing 3 TDs in the first quarter and a total of 5 in the game in a 42–20 blowout against the Niners. After four games, he had thrown 14 TDs, 2 more TDs than the Rams had through all last season, and a QB rating of 136.0.

Around this time, *Sports Illustrated* featured the article, "Who Is This Guy?" It was so shocking that this nobody—Kurt Warner—took the NFL by storm. The article was very appropriately titled because going into the season, he seemed like just a guy and not an NFL quarterback. For one, he played Division 1-AA ball from the University of Northern Iowa; he also had two failed attempts at the NFL; he was stocking shelves at Hy-Vee grocery store in his hometown in Iowa; and he had a brief stint in Arena League football with the Iowa Barnstormers. A guy with this background is setting unheard of numbers. Prior to the '99 season, he played in only one NFL game. You just have to ask, "Who *is* this guy? *Where* did he come from? *What the heck is going on?*"

The article also touched on what kind of person he is outside of football. Kurt Warner was a man of faith. He always has had strong Christian beliefs. I think his rise came as a surprise to everybody—except him. When asked, "What is the secret to your success?" he replied, "My faith in Jesus Christ." His unwavering faith in the Lord gave him the confidence to lead his own life on his terms, as demonstrated on the football field.

The article described him as the anti-Ryan Leaf. He wasn't drafted early; he was handed nothing; he made the league minimum for a second-year player of $250,000/year and was content with making that money; and also, unlike Ryan Leaf, he showed good results. No one was more grateful to play the game than Kurt Warner.

As the next few weeks rolled on, the Rams, 6–0, would face their future Super Bowl opponent, the Tennessee Titans. This would be the low point of the season as they lost a close one, 24–21, submitting 21 points in the first quarter. They made a good comeback. Warner still had 328 passing yards, but ultimately, they came up short.

The next week, the Rams would lose again in another close battle, 31–27. Warner, again, had a good a game; it just wasn't enough. At this point, writers and the general public didn't believe the big hype anymore about the Rams. They thought maybe the clock had struck midnight on Warner's Cinderella Story. It made sense that Warner's dominance was too good to be true.

He came back from those two losses very strong. He would win seven straight after those two losses.

◄ **THE GREATEST SHOW ON TURF**

They won the division and home field throughout the playoffs. He would finish the regular season with 4,353 yards and 41 TDs, leading the league in both categories and earning a league MVP, and would eventually earn the Super Bowl MVP.

It was the postseason where he really proved that he was lights out. The first game against the Vikings was a shoot-out. It was like watching a track meet. The very first offensive play for the Rams, Warner connected with Bruce on a 77-yard TD pass. By the end of the play, there were no defenders around, just a convoy of Rams' receivers running with Bruce. The second possession, the Rams struck quick again with a short pass to Faulk and ended up in a 41-yard TD pass. In the end, Warner threw 5 TD passes to 5 different receivers, winning 49–37.

Game two was actually a very defensive game. It was an ugly performance on Warner's part, throwing three interceptions prior to his final drive. The Rams were down 6–5 on the 30-yard line with 4 minutes remaining. As a fan, you are expecting Bruce, Holt, Faulk, or at the very least, Hakim, to get the ball. Warner surprised everybody when he heaved up the ball to Ricky Proehl, a man who didn't have any TDs all season. As the ball was coming down and very close to the sideline, that was who the Rams were depending on—Ricky Proehl. Somehow, Warner knew what he was doing because Proehl pulled that ball in with an amazing catch to win the game. It was an unconventional game for the Rams statistically as the offense played subpar, but prior to the catch, Proehl was pretty much the only one having a solid game, and Warner must have known he would have the best chance at that ball.

Warner had one more clutch performance in the Super Bowl. With the game tied at 16 on the final drive for the Rams, he connected with Isaac Bruce on a 73-yard TD pass to take the lead 23–16. Warner also set a Super Bowl record for passing yards: 414.

He would continue on the fast track in 2000. He started 6–0, throwing 300 yards again in every game, 19 TDs, which was a better start than the previous year. Warner got hurt in the seventh game, and Trent Green did a great job as his backup. They combined 5,492 passing yards, which is an NFL team record. Warner finished the season with 21 TD passes and once again earned a spot in the Pro Bowl. The offense might have been even better than the previous year, but the difference was

◄ THE GREATEST SHOW ON TURF

that the defense was horrendous.

Kurt had another MVP season in 2001, throwing 36 TDs. He had a tendency of throwing more interceptions that year, but overall, it was a great year. He started 6–0 for the third straight year, and there was, once again, a major buzz about how unstoppable Warner was. At this point, he was more than a Cinderella Story or perennial starter or Pro Bowler. He was the dominant force of the NFL. Warner remained solid through the playoffs and, once more, had a terrific Super Bowl, throwing for 377 yards, which, at the time, was second-most number of yards thrown in Super Bowl history, only losing to his own previous Super Bowl record.

In 2002, as the Rams declined, so did Warner as Marc Bulger emerged and Warner's new role was Bulger's mentor. At this point, I considered the mini era of "The Greatest Show On Turf" over. I'm not taking anything away from Bulger because he is a good QB, and he almost saved the Rams' '02 season, and he had a successful '03 season, but they were declining. I do think the Rams made a good choice in going with Bulger, for whatever reason. Warner just hit a slump that lasted about 4 years.

Warner had a few seasons on the bench and

KURT WARNER

other mediocre seasons between one year with the New York Giants and a few with the Arizona Cardinals. During the '07 season and especially '08 season, he revived his career. He led the Cardinals to a Super Bowl and almost won. People no longer say he was a fluke or that he was in the right place in a great system. Warner made a legitimate case for being a future Hall of Famer.

He started his career proving he was worthy of being in the NFL, and now he is proving he deserves to be in the Hall of Fame.

				Kurt Warner stats '99–'01			
Yr.	Cmp	Att	Cmp%	Yds	TDs	Int	QB Rtg
'99	325	499	65.1	4,353	41	13	109.2
'00	235	347	67.7	3,429	21	18	98.3
'01	375	546	68.7	4,830	36	22	101.4

		Kurt Warner career stats			
Cmp	Att	Cmp%	Yds.	Td	Int
2327	3557	65.4	28,591	182	114

Marshall Faulk

Marshall Faulk was definitely the workhorse of the Ram's offense. One might ask, where does a halfback fit into a spread offense? Actually, they probably have the most important role on the team. He acted as a receiver and frequently led the league in receiving for halfbacks. When it came time to run, he was no slouch either. He had elusive speed and finesse. Defenses usually weren't prepared for the run, and he would add another dimension to the offense.

For 3 years, the argument was, who is more valuable to the team, Warner or Faulk? They were both putting up MVP numbers, and both times, Warner won the MVP, Faulk was second but was offensive MVP 3 years in a row, and he earned the league MVP himself in 2000. Another fact to

◄ **THE GREATEST SHOW ON TURF**

remember when it comes to the Rams' success is that the Rams were 27–1 when Faulk had over 100 yards rushing, winning 25 consecutive games. He was the main ingredient for success. Give Faulk the ball = 96 percent chance of winning.

When the Rams acquired Faulk in 1999, the Rams' franchise looked like it was going to make a turn. I don't know if anybody expected these results, but picking up the best halfback in the game was a heck of a start. He had turned the Colts around and had a NFL record of four consecutive seasons in which he managed to gain 2,000 yards from scrimmage per season. It was time to bring that magic to St. Louis.

I would say that Faulk's season started off a little slow in '99 as far as rushing goes, but the thing about Faulk is that no one shut him down completely. He was always a factor. He was either a threat in rushing or receiving, and sometimes he was both, and that was just too hard to stop. He would eventually pick up his running game. Around midseason, he was hot as he had four straight 100-yard rushing games consecutive. That season, he had seven 100-yard rushing games and one 200-yard receiving game against the Bears. He totaled 1,381 yards rushing and 1,048 yards receiving

MARSHALL FAULK

and 12 TDs, 7 rushing and 5 receiving.

In the playoffs, his rushing stats were less than mediocre as the Rams were throwing a lot through the playoffs. He sure made up for it in receiving. He opened the Viking game wide open with a little shovel pass to him. He burned that defense to make the score 14–3, and he had a rushing TD in that game. He ended up with 80 yards receiving that game. When it came to the Super Bowl, he had 90 yards receiving, so he was absolutely instrumental through the playoffs.

In 2000, he would have an even more impressive season, setting the NFL record of total TDs in a season. The remarkable thing is how he did it in actually 14 games as he missed two games due to injury.

The most impressive game in the season is when they played New Orleans' final game of the season. If the Rams won, they would clinch a wildcard spot. Faulk absolutely thrashed the defense for 220 yards rushing and a total of 3 TDs. This was the second time this season he rushed over 200 yards, as when he did it against the Falcons in week 7.

Faulk would finish the season with 18 rushing TDs and 8 receiving TDs, 1,359 rushing yards, and 830 yards receiving, totaling 2,189 yards from

THE GREATEST SHOW ON TURF

scrimmage. He would add a league MVP and another offensive MVP to his accomplishments.

In 2001, Faulk had another great 14-game season. This year he was involved in a running back duo with Trung Canidate. Canidate looked like a young promising halfback when he filled in for Faulk. Believe it or not, he actually led Faulk in yards per carry, but Faulk was like superman. He didn't need a sidekick. Again, Faulk rushed for over 1,300 yards for the third straight time with the Rams. He actually beat his rushing total in '99 by one yard, having 1,382 yards. He had 765 yards receiving with 8 TDs and 12 rushing TDs. He was second to Warner again in the MVP running, but once again, he earned offensive MVP.

Faulk had a bigger role in the playoffs this time, especially in the NFC Championship, rushing for 159 yards and having 2 TDs in a close 29–24 victory to make their second Super Bowl in 3 years.

Now Faulk has his number retired with the Rams and is ranked fourth in yards from scrimmage and ninth in rushing yards. He is, without a doubt, a future Hall of Famer.

MARSHALL FAULK

			Marshall Faulk Stats '99–'01			
		Rushing			Receiving	
Yr	Att	Yds	TDs	Rec	Yds	TDs
'99	253	1,381	7	87	1,048	5
'00	253	1,359	18	81	830	8
'01	260	1,382	12	83	765	9

Marshall Faulk career stats		
Att	Yds	Td
2836	12,279	100

Marshall Faulk career receiving stats		
Rec	Yds	Td
767	6875	36

The Defense

The defense was highly underrated. In fact, when people said "The Greatest Show On Turf," it had nothing to do with the defense. What many people don't realize is that in '99 and '01, that defense was quick, just like the offense. They were quick to get the quarterback, and when they forced turnovers, they were quick to return it for many yards, and quite a few TDs.

On the frontline, you had Kevin Carter, D'Marco Farr, and Grant Wistrom. Kevin Carter that season had 17 sacks and led the league. D'Marco Farr had 8.5 sacks while Wistrom and Leonard Little were still young, Wistrom returned a couple TDs, one on an interception while the other was a fumble recovery. Little would emerge the next year since he was suspended for a drunken driving incident.

The one thing that added to the Rams' speed on defense was turning Leonard Little from linebacker to defensive end. He was a bit undersized for a lineman, which helped because he was always much quicker than the offensive line. In 2000, in that role, he had five sacks and got better every year. The following year, he had 14.5 sacks, which ranked third in the NFL.

Then there were the linebackers who were led by London Fletcher at middle linebacker. In 2000, he had 5.5 sacks, 4 interceptions, and 106 tackles. He was just all over the place. On the left side, Mike Jones had a very surprising year in '99. He might have only been a 1-year wonder, but to have a year like that is something to proud of. He returned 4 interceptions for 96 yards, 2 of them were TDs. He recovered 2 fumbles for 52 yards, and another TD, totaling 3 defensive TDs.

Despite that great season, he is still defined by *one* moment, and that was the very last play of the Super Bowl. The Rams were up 23–16, the defense was exhausted because the Titans drove all the way down the field and had the ball on the 6-yard line with only time for one more play. If you watch the footage of the final drive, you will see Carter and

THE DEFENSE

Farr asking Vermeil to be subbed—that is how tired the defense was. Vermeil responded with "You gotta be kidding me!!! *It's the Super Bowl!*"

With all that huffing and puffing, McNair took the snap, threw a quick slant over the middle to Kevin Dyson, and it looked as if he was going to make it—until Mike Jones made a heroic tackle to win the game on the 1-yard line. After the blue and yellow confetti cleared and Warner was named MVP, everyone remembered that offense, but that play, and even that game, showed that defense was equally important. They always held opponents to low scores and made big plays when they had to.

The defensive backs were something to see also. Rookie Dré Bly was the nickel back. Dexter McCleon and Todd Lyght were the two corners. Todd Lyght, just like Mike Jones, had his breakout season in '99. He had 6 interceptions returned for 112 yards and 1 touchdown. Bly, for a rookie nickel back having 3 interceptions, returning 1 for a touchdown, is pretty good. He was also a good contribution to special teams. Dexter McCleon pulled off 4 interceptions that year.

In a couple years when they added veteran Aeneas Williams, they were just awesome. When he intercepted the ball, there was a good chance he

THE GREATEST SHOW ON TURF

would take it all the way. Brett Favre would find that in the 2001–02 playoff. He returned 2 interceptions for 2 touchdowns in that game. The Rams' defense really rattled Favre as they picked him off six times and proved the Packer receivers were not a match for the DBs on the Rams.

The very next game, the NFC Championship, he put the exclamation on the Rams' win when he intercepted the ball with less than 2 minutes to go. That's another game where you remember Faulk or Warner's performance, but it was the defense that won the game in the end.

Williams later moved to safety, where he played okay, but he finally hung up the cleats in '04. At safety, they had Keith Lyle, Devin Bush, and later, Adam Archuleta and Kim Herring. Archuleta was a linebacker in college, and the Rams turned him into a safety. He wasn't that fast, but he could hit hard. I wouldn't want to go up for a ball when he was near. He was also a threat to the quarterback as he blitzed quite often.

Herring was a part of the 2000 Ravens, which was the greatest defense to ever play. He was a solid starter. Bush and Lyle both had 2 interceptions apiece in '99, despite both of them only playing half the season. Lyle had a few great years before

THE DEFENSE

'99, once leading the league in interceptions with 9 in '96.

Aside from 2000, the '99 and '01 Rams were dominating. In '99, they only allowed 15 points a game, led the league in sacks with 57, allowed only 74 rushing yards a game, and had an amazing 8 TDs returned, 7 on interceptions and 1 fumble recovery. Five different defensive players scored: Jones, Wistrom, Lyght, Bush, and Bly. I also believe that the defense was responsible for winning the NFC Championship Game, and the Super Bowl was won by the defense on the final play.

In '01, the defense only allowed 17 points a game, and that is good considering the year before they allowed 29 points a game. They also had 5 TDs returned, 4 off of interceptions and 1 off a fumble recovery. They had 45 sacks. This defense played strong in the playoffs, especially against Green Bay, but the Rams were firing from all cylinders. I don't thing that in the Super Bowl the offense played to their full potential until it was too late. No one can argue with how the defense played that Super Bowl against New England.

Dick Vermeil

Dick Vermeil is notoriously known for his working long hours and burning out in his first stint as a head coach. The phrase "gotta go to work" was coined by Dick Vermeil, and he lived it every day. In the late '70s and early '80s as Eagles' head coach, he worked 16-hour days as the head coach, offensive coordinator, and QB coach. He did it all—and slept in his office. He was known for pushing his players as hard as he worked. In the end, he, and the players, just burned out. When the Eagles lost in the Super Bowl to the Raiders, many players said they were just tired due to being pushed so hard all the time. This loss, accompanied by his physical and emotional exhaustion, forced Vermeil to retire from coaching in 1983.

In 1997, he was called by John Shaw to help

rebuild the St. Louis Rams. In the '90s, up to the point of Vermeil taking over the Rams, they had 36 wins and 76 losses. His job was to take the little bit of talent they had and work them hard and turn them into winners.

The training camp consisted of a 3-hour practice in the morning and 3 hours at night. It was always full pads and full contact. All that in the August heat would either make the team as tough as nails, or it could risk breaking them down completely. In '98 is when many players started to rebel against Vermeil and complain about working too hard. They could barely walk because they were sore all over. It was a very slow and painful process and seemed unsuccessful in the first 2 years of his campaign.

However, in '99, all that work paid out big dividends. He worked a group of guys as hard as he could for as long as he could and then eased up on them in '99. Practice went from 3 hours to 1½ hours. The players had reached their peak condition from prior sessions with Vermeil. Now it was time to rest those muscles and stay healthy and put that work on the field. Spending 2 years getting those guys fit was a great strategy. That's why they were one of the fastest teams on both sides of the ball. They just *never* got tired!

To me, Vermeil seems like a friend first, coach second. Maybe even a father figure to a team. He may push and yell, but deep down, he loves his players. He can't hide it either. He cries a lot. He can be hard as nails or soft as a pillow. Anytime you see him in a press conference, it's an emotional moment. He is almost sure to cry and share his love with his fellow team members.

Mike Martz

Behind every great man, team, or master plan, there is a master mind. That is what Mike Martz was to the St. Louis Rams. He was discovered in Washington when he had success as the QB coach, and he was then called to the St. Louis Rams to be the offensive coordinator. The team and the staff were the puppets, and Martz was pulling the strings. While Vermeil was a natural leader who was the motivator, Martz was the X's and O's coach. I believe it was Vermeil who was able to condition the team to get fast and durable, but it was Martz who utilized that talent right.

He had the perfect style offense for the type speed team that he had. It was a spread West Coast offense. The offense relied on spreading all five receivers out into patterns which stretched the field. This forced defensive backs to cover receivers on timing routes in which the quarterback would throw to a spot where the receiver could catch the ball and turn upfield.

Pass protection is critical to success because at least two of the five receivers will run a deep in, skinny post, comeback, speed out, or shallow cross. Mike Martz credits the offensive system as being influenced by Sid Gillman and refined by NFL coach Don Coryell. Martz learned the so-called 3-digit system the offense is famous for from Norv Turner when they were both in Washington. The Rams set a new NFL record for total offensive yards in 2000, with 7,335, and 5,492 of those being passing yards. It was a new NFL team record.

Martz also has been credited with turning no-name quarterbacks into the league's best. Warner, Green, and Bulger all can thank Martz for the jump start to their great careers.

Martz had a presence to him that seemed very calm, cool, and collected. He would never get overemotional or excited. He was like Dick Vermeil's exact opposite. Sometimes his swagger was mistaken for arrogance. Rams' fans either loved him or hated him. Fans of other teams *definitely* hated him. The aggressive play calling tended to be a bit passing friendly. Many felt he underused the talent of Faulk and later Jackson. I disagree. He turned Faulk into a very effective receiver, and when he ran, it surprised teams and would lead to big gains by Faulk. Defenses had a hard enough time with Rams' receivers, and then they had to watch the backfield as well for shovel passes or halfback screens.

Some would argue that the Martz team in '01 might have been better than the '99 team led by Vermeil. The only difference is that championship ring. You could also argue that if not for the Patriots' spy gating scandal, the Rams might have that ring. The 2000 team certainly looked the best in the league until injuries hit them. The Rams could have been the dynasty while Patriots might not have had their success.

Towards the '04 season and '05 season, Rams' fans hated Mike Martz so much they started a Web site, www.firemikemartz.com. Even if you were part of that group, I still don't think you can deny the success that Martz had. He had four playoff appearances in five full seasons, a record of 56–36, which is .600 winning percentage, three playoff victories as head coach, a Super Bowl appearance, a Super Bowl victory as an offensive coordinator, and was the last Rams' coach to actually have a winning record. So say what you want to say about Mike Martz, but the Rams haven't been the same since he left.

Ricky Proehl

Ricky Proehl was absolutely instrumental to the team's success because he added depth to the wide receivers. The Rams had two of the best receivers in Bruce and Holt, a great third option in Hakim, but Proehl was not an obvious choice—which made him dangerous. When you double cover Bruce, man up on Holt, crowd the box on Faulk, who is left to watch Proehl and Hakim? The answer is *no one*. They are wide open, and Proehl has great hands.

Proehl's biggest contribution came in the NFC Championship Game against the Tampa Bay Buccaneers. While the Rams were being shut down for the first time the whole season, Proehl was the only one who was effective. He caught six passes for a hundred yards and the game-winning touchdown in the final 5 minutes of the game, to win 11–6.

◂ THE GREATEST SHOW ON TURF

The amazing thing is how Proehl caught that pass. It was a last-ditch effort for the Rams, and Warner heaved it up. It looked as though he were throwing it away. All of a sudden, in the front corner of the end zone, Proehl planted his feet, reached up, and pulled that ball in for the touchdown.

Two years later, he kept the Rams alive in the Super Bowl against the Patriots, tying the game on a big catch, 17–17, with 1:30 minutes to go. It was, however, a losing effort.

Proehl went on to more successes after the Rams: a Super Bowl ring with the Colts and a Super Bowl appearance with the Carolina Panthers. He had another big touchdown with the Panthers in the Super Bowl. He was just a big-game clutch kind of guy, a very useful weapon to the arsenal. He is like the handgun you would keep in your pant leg during battle. In a worst-case scenario when out of weapons, he was extremely handy.

In his 5 years as a Ram, he had 207 receptions for 2,590 yards. He would retire after 16 seasons in the NFL, two Super Bowl rings, and four Super Bowl appearances with three different teams. That fact right there tells you that he is a *key part* to the success of any team he plays for.

RICKY PROEHL

	Ricky Proehl		
Yr	Rec	Yds	Td
99	33	349	0
00	31	441	4
01	40	563	5

Ricky Proehl Career Stats		
Rec	Yds	Td
669	8879	54

Az-Zahir Hakim/Tony Horne/ Special Teams

Aside from being a punt return specialist, Hakim was a very acrobatic, speedy receiver. Drafted in the fourth round from San Diego State in the '98 draft, I'm not sure anyone expected big things from him in only his second year. In '99, he really came on the scene as a key player.

October, 3, 1999, Hakim had a career day against the Cincinnati Bengals. He became the fourth Ram in history to score 4 touchdowns in one game. One was an 84-yard punt return. The punt return was the fifth longest in franchise history and the third longest of the '99 season around the league. He also set a team record with 147 punt return yards in a game. Against the Atlanta Falcons,

◀ THE GREATEST SHOW ON TURF

Hakim had another memorable day, having 3 receptions, all for touchdowns. He was a huge factor in the division clincher game against the Panthers, scoring 2 touchdowns on four catches and having his first 100-yard receiving game. He finished the season with 677 receiving yards and 8 receiving TDs, which was second on the team in TD's, only behind Isaac Bruce.

The season 2000 started off with a bang on a Monday night showdown with the Denver Broncos. With five catches, Hakim racked up 116 yards and 2 TDs. Three Rams had over a hundred yards that game, and Hakim was one of them, and he returned an 86-yard punt. Statistically speaking, his 2000 season was a little bit better than the '99 season. Unfortunately, the season ended on a bad note for him in the playoffs against the New Orleans Saints. In what looked like was going to be an impressive comeback for the Rams, Hakim muffed a punt to lose the game.

Hakim finished the season leading the NFC in punt return average with 15.8 yard per average. When he left the Rams, he had 1,000 punt return yards, a feat that only three Rams have accomplished, and he holds the franchise record for most punt return yards as a Ram.

AZ-ZAHIR HAKIM/TONY HORNE/SPECIAL TEAMS

	Az-Zahir Hakim		
Yr	Rec	Yds	Td
99	36	677	8
00	53	734	4
01	39	374	3

Az-zahir Hakim Career Stats		
Rec	Yds	Td
316	4,191	28

Az-Zahir Hakim Punt Return Stats			
Yr	Pr	Yds	Td
99	44	461	1
00	32	489	1
01	36	330	0

Tony Horne

Horne had a very significant role on special teams. He never got much action as a receiver, but he definitely helped through this role. He had a very short career, shortened by an injury. In '99, he had two kick returns returned for a touchdown, not including one he had in the playoffs against the Vikings. He finished his career with 4 TDs and 1 playoff TD in only 3 years of playing. In '98 and '00, he returned over 1,300 yards, and in '99, 29.7 yards per return, which was his season high.

The combination of Hakim and Horne returning was deadly. If they didn't score, they gave the offense a short field to work with. Between the two of them, they saw 7 career touchdown returns and 2,200 yards returned. That is a major contributor to their success.

◀ THE GREATEST SHOW ON TURF

	Tony Horne Kick Return Stats		
Yr	Ret	Yds	Td
99	30	892	2
00	57	1,379	1
Tony Horne Career Kick Return Stats			
Ret	Yds	TD	
143	3,577	4	

Isaac Bruce

Before the '99 season, Isaac Bruce was the Rams only offensive weapon. In '94, he was drafted in the second round from the University of Memphis to the Los Angeles Rams. He was in L.A. and St. Louis through all the bad years in the '90s. That, however, didn't stop him from working hard and putting up good stats. When the team wasn't doing so hot, Isaac made the Pro Bowl in '96 and was an alternate in '95, only his second season as a Ram. It was discovered quickly that he was the only offensive weapon in the mid-90s, so this new team direction was built around speedy receivers. This was a trend that Bruce started.

The echoes of the word "Bruuuuuuuuuccee" was all over St. Louis when Bruce made a big play. If one weren't a fan, they might think that he was being booed in the stadium. Isaac was a very speedy receiver, at a very trim 188 lbs. Many defensive backs had a hard time keeping up with Isaac; he would burn them and just leave them in the dust. When '99 came, his best years were yet to come.

The new put-together team would really compliment his style, as it promised an air assault on the defenses. Isaac was supposed to be the center that this team was building around. As the team leader, he was very frustrated with losing. He would get very critical of other players' performances. He had every right to. I think he showed leadership, and it would bring the best out of his players.

Vermeil and Bruce butted heads on this issue as Vermeil commented, "Bruce is not paid to evaluate and coach; he is paid to play." Bruce took great offense to that comment by Vermeil. Bruce was very passionate about the game, as made obvious by his frustration that would come out, like the time Green was hurt. It was Bruce who was at centerfield who threw his helmet down and punched the turf.

When '99 came around and there were new receivers in town and a new QB, Bruce exploded on the field with huge numbers. Only this time, he would have a little help from his supporting cast. With Bruce, they were a team that you needed to

ISAAC BRUCE

watch out for one day, and when the other additions came to the team, they became the team you feared. As the leader of the team and key receiver, he racked up 1,000-plus yards in four straight seasons as a Ram between '99–'02. It would only be appropriate that Bruce would make the winning catch and run to win Super Bowl XXXIV.

The Titans were making what seemed to be a great Super Bowl comeback as they tied the game at 16–16. With 2 minutes remaining in the game, the Rams took the field at their own 27-yard line. In the first play of the drive, Warner threw a bomb as it was up in the air. Bruce was one on one with Denard Walker. Bruce saw that the ball was slightly underthrown as he hit his brakes; Walker kept going forward. Bruce then made the grab and sidestepped Walker as he fell to the ground. He pulled off another juke and headed to the end zone to take the lead 23–16. That was Bruce's greatest moment in his outstanding career with the Rams.

Bruce got the ball rolling for the Rams and became a great mentor for Torry Holt. He was the team leader prior to that season, then new leaders would emerge, but it was Bruce that got the Rams on track. He now is in the latter years of his career with the rival 49ers. He is second for all-time

◀ THE GREATEST SHOW ON TURF

receiving yards with 1,000 career receptions. He has been named to four Pro Bowls, was once a Pro Bowl alternate, and, of course, has a Super Bowl ring which he earned by contributing to the biggest offensive play of the game.

	Issac Bruce		
yr	Rec	Yds	Tds
99	77	1,165	12
00	87	1,471	9
01	64	1,106	6

Isaac Bruce Career Stats		
Rec	Yds	Td
1,003	14,944	91

Torry Holt

The youngest of the receivers was just a rookie in '99 and was, perhaps, the most promising. He was like Bruce. He stood at 6' even, weighed 190 lbs, and he could run the 40-yard dash in 4.38 seconds. He was the receiver that had a chance to actually to keep up with Bruce. He was drafted the sixth overall pick in the '99 draft from North Carolina State. He brought hope to the city of St. Louis with his addition to the team. Fans knew they had Green, Faulk, and Bruce. Now, the hottest receiver in college was going to upgrade that offense. I guess you could say he was that final piece to that offense. That was the objective when the Rams' management spoke to Vermeil.

As the protégé of Isaac Bruce, he took what he was taught to another level. The '99 season was a learning season, but he didn't have many growing pains. Twice that season, he had 100-yard games, and twice, he had multiple touchdown games. He really picked up his stride toward the last five games of the season, and that is when you just *knew* he was going to be something. He finished that season with 788 yards and 6 TDs.

During Super Bowl XXXIV, he scored a key touchdown late in the third quarter to extend the lead to 16–0 against the Titans.

At NC State, Holt earned the nickname "Big Game." He carried it through the NFL as two of his biggest games in '99 were in the postseason. As mentioned before, he had a touchdown in the Super Bowl, and in the divisional game against the Vikings, he had another TD. He amassed 242 yards, 2 TDs, and 20 receptions in the 3 games of '99 postseason. Now, put those stats aside and think about his regular season. Compared to what he did in the postseason, 788 yards and 6 TDs in sixteen regular season games is very mediocre. As mentioned earlier, it took him about 10 games to take off and become an impact player, and it carried through just in time through the postseason.

After establishing himself in '99, Holt went six consecutive seasons with 1,400 yards, which is an

TORRY HOLT

NFL record. He ranks among the top 10 active leaders in receiving yards, receiving touchdowns and receptions, and has finished in the top ten of those three categories in each of the last five seasons (2003–2007). Holt has also led the league in receiving yardage on two separate occasions (2000, 2003), and receptions once (2003). Holt is nearing the top ten for all-time receiving yards. He currently ranks 11th. Holt was also the fastest player to reach 10,000 yards, achieving this in only his sixth season, and is a 7-time Pro Bowler. This is what he leaves behind as he ventures off to the Jaguars. He had a great 10 years with the Rams and was the last original member of "The Greatest Show On Turf" to leave town.

	Torry Holt		
yr	Rec	Yds	Td
99	52	788	6
00	82	1,635	6
01	81	1,363	7
	Torry Holt Career Stats		
Rec	Yds	Td	
869	12,660	74	

The Legacy

What do the Rams leave behind with all this? They weren't a dynasty; they barely qualify as an era. They are a mini era, if you will. What they leave behind is that for a period of 3 years, they were the greatest offense in the league. Looking back in history, they are the greatest offense to ever lace up their cleats. They were, without a doubt, the fastest all-around team ever assembled. According to the NFL Network, they were ranked number 19 of the greatest Super Bowl Championships. Marshall Faulk, who works with the Network, disagrees and says they are number 1. I do disagree with 19, although maybe number 1 is being a little too generous. It's hard to argue against the '85 Bears or the '72 Dolphins, but I think third or fourth is a fair number.

THE GREATEST SHOW ON TURF

Had they won the second Super Bowl, we would be talking about a dynasty. They would be what the Patriots are to the 2000s, the Cowboys of the '90s, the 49ers of the '80s, and so on. I always think about the possibilities and what if the Patriots just played for overtime at the end of the game? Or what if there had been no spy gating on the Patriots' side? How would we look at the Rams now? I know that I could compare that '99 team to any of the Steelers, Cowboys, or 49ers team that won the big one. The '01 could be compared, even if they don't have the ring.

In the end, "The Greatest Show On Turf" was great, but one more Super Bowl, and they could have been legendary. It is fun to think what could have been.

THE LEGACY

Week	Opponent	Result
1	Bal	27–10 W
3	Atl	35–7 W
4	At Cin	38–10 W
5	SF	42–20 W
6	At Atl	41–13 W
7	Cle	34–3 W
8	At Ten	24–21 L
9	At Det	31–27 L
10	Car	35–10 W
11	At SF	23–7 W
12	NO	43–12 W
13	At Car	34–21 W
14	At NO	30–14 W
15	NYG	31–10 W
16	Chi	34–12 W
17	Phi	34–13 L

99 Postseason

	Opponent	Result
Divisional	Min	49–27 W
NFC Championship	TB	11–6 W
Super Bowl XXXIV	Ten	23–16 W

◄ THE GREATEST SHOW ON TURF

- Led NFL in total yards (400.8 yards per game)
- Led NFL in passing yards (272.1 yards per game)
- Led NFL in scoring (32.9 points per game)
- Led NFL in rushing defense (74.3 yards per game)
- Led NFL (tied with Jax) in sacks (57)

2000 Season		
Week	Opponent	Result
1	Den	41–36 W
2	At Sea	37–34 W
3	SF	41–24 W
4	At Atl	41–20 W
5	Sd	57–31 W
6		
7	Atl	45–29 W
8	At Kc	54–34 L
9	At SF	34–24 W
10	Car	37–24 L
11	At Nyg	38–24 W
12	Was	33–20 L
13	No	31–24 L
14	At Car	16–3 L
15	Min	40–29 W
16	At Tb	38–35 L
17	At No	26–21 W

2000 Postseason	
Opponent	Result
At No	31–28 L

THE LEGACY

- Led NFL avg yards per play (7.0)
- Led NFL combined net yards gained (7,075)
- Led NFL first downs, passing (247 first downs)
- Led NFL net yards (5,232)
- Led NFL passes completed (380)
- Led NFL passing offense
- Led NFL passing TDs (37)
- Led NFL percentage of passes completed (64.7 percent)
- Led NFL rushing TDs (26)
- Led NFL third-down efficiency (47.5 percent of third downs converted)
- Led NFL total offense
- Led NFL total TDs (67)
- Led NFL yards gained per completed pass (14.5) yards
- Only team to have three straight seasons to start 6–0

◄ THE GREATEST SHOW ON TURF

	2001 Season	
Week	Opponent	Result
1	At Phi	20–17 W
2	At SF	30–26 W
3	Mia	42–10 W
4	At Det	35–0 W
5	Nyg	15–14 W
6	At Nyj	34–14 W
7	No	34–31 L
8	Bye	
9	Car	48–14 W
10	At Ne	24–17 W
11	Tb	24–17 L
12	At Atl	35–6 W
13	SF	27–14 W
14	At No	34–21 W
15	At Car	38–32 W
16	Ind	42–17 W
17	Atl	31–13 W
2001 Postseason		
Opponent	Result	
Gb Div	45–17 W	
Phi NFC Championship	29–24 W	
Ne SuperBowl XXXVI	20–17 L	

- Only team to score 500 points in three straight seasons
- League MVP Kurt Warner
- Offensive MVP Marshall Faulk
- Three consecutive seasons with the MVP (99,00,01)

Lightning Source UK Ltd.
Milton Keynes UK
11 December 2009

147361UK00001B/85/P